Different Kinds of Families

Sharon K. Kittle

the Peppertree Press
Sarasota, Florida

This Book Belongs To:

_____

Copyright © Sharon K. Kittle, 2014

All rights reserved. Published by the Peppertree Press, LLC. the Peppertree Press and associated logos are trademarks of the Peppertree Press, LLC.

No part of this publication may be reproduced, stored in a retrieval system, transmitted in any form or by any means, electronic, mechanical, photocopying, recording, or otherwise, without prior written permission of the publisher and author/illustrator. Graphic design by Rebecca Barbier.

For information regarding permission,
call 941-922-2662 or contact us at our website:
www.peppertreepublishing.com or write to:
the Peppertree Press, LLC.
Attention: Publisher
1269 First Street, Suite 7
Sarasota, Florida 34236

ISBN: 978-1-61493-262-8

Library of Congress Number: 2014907508

Printed in the U.S.A.

Printed May 2014

Dedicated to Steven Reeves. We miss you.

There are many types of families
Who reside along my street.
Let's look at them together
For a little meet and greet.

First there is my family.
It's me, my mom, and dad,
My baby sister, Catherine,
And Boots, my fat old cat.

Next door to me is Franklin.
He has a mom and brother.
His dad lives in another town,
But they often see each other.

Cora Jane lives with two dads.
She has a doll named Emily.
They seem to laugh and play a lot.
She's happy with her family.

Lexi lives with Grammy Midge.
They seem to like it that way.
Their house smells good because they bake.
We eat cupcakes and then we play.

Matthew, Donohue and Drew
Are my very closest buds.
They have two moms
Named Syd and Chris
Who let them stomp in the mud.

Lucy's parents are different too.
Dad's skin is light; Mom's is dark.
I didn't even consider it though
Until I heard it said in the park.

Freddo's mommy came from Spain,
But his daddy was born in the states.
Once a week he plays with his sitter
So his parents can go out on their date.

Jilly has a lot of brothers.
She has many sisters too.

Her parents are very busy with them.
They call their family the 'Zoo.'

Lily came on a plane from China
To meet her new mom and dad.
She loves her life in their little house
And I've never seen her sad.

Rosie's in a wheelchair,
But she plays right along with us.
She lives with her dad, Peter
And she rides to school on our bus.

Annabel's mom married Suzy's dad.
They blended two families into one.
Now Annabel and Suzy are best friends
And their days are filled with fun.

We all have different families
And yet we are also the same.
We live with people
Who love one another
And that will never change.

Other Titles by Sharon K. Kittle

The Really Read Book

978-1-61493-235-2 (hardcover)	$22.95
978-1-61493-234-5 (paperback)	$12.95

There's a book in my house that I keep by my bed. It's my very favorite book and it's really, really read.

Pirate Play Day

978-1-61493-259-8 (hardcover)	$22.95
978-1-61493-258-1 (paperback)	$12.95

Follow an imaginative boy through his day as he plays adventurous little pirate.

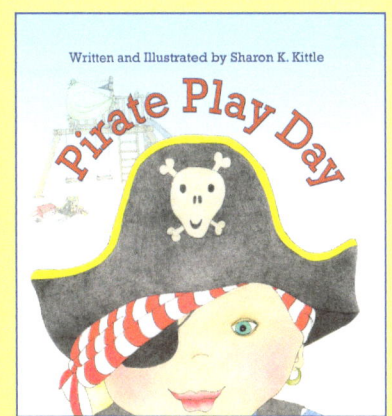

Flit the Fly Travels the Sky

978-1-61493-241-3 (hardcover)	$22.95
978-1-61493-242-0 (paperback)	$12.95

Mom's Choice Award winner, *Flit the Fly* is a mesmerizing geography lesson for eager toddlers, who won't realize they are actually learning as they have fun following Flit's travels from place to place.

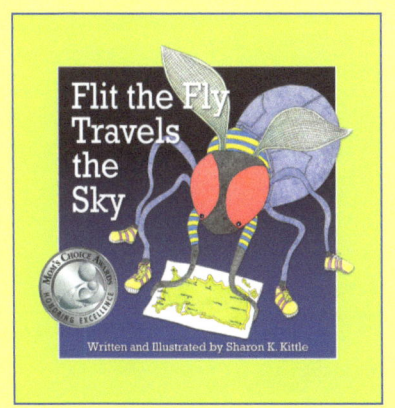

www.ingramcontent.com/pod-product-compliance
Ingram Content Group UK Ltd.
Pitfield, Milton Keynes, MK11 3LW, UK
UKHW061645240426
12048UKWH00036B/5